Passive Income

The Ultimate Guide to Financial Freedom

© Copyright 2016 by DCB Web Trading Ltd _____ - All rights reserved.

This document is presented with the desire to provide reliable, quality information about the topic in question and the facts discussed within. This eBook is sold under the assumption that neither the author nor the publisher should be asked to provide the services discussed within. If any discussion, professional or legal, is otherwise required a proper professional should be consulted.

This Declaration was held acceptable and equally approved by the Committee of Publishers and Associations as well as the American Bar Association.

The reproduction, duplication or transmission of any of the included information is considered illegal whether done in print or electronically. Creating a recorded copy or a secondary copy of this work is also prohibited unless the action of doing so is first cleared through the Publisher and condoned in writing. All rights reserved.

Any information contained in the following pages is considered accurate and truthful and that any liability through inattention or by any use or misuse of the topics discussed within falls solely on the reader. There are no cases in which the Publisher of this work can be held responsible or be asked to provide reparations for any loss of monetary gain or other damages which may be caused by following the presented information in any way shape or form.

The following information is presented purely for informative purposes and is therefore considered universal. The information presented within is done so without a contract or any other type of assurance as to its quality or validity.

Any trademarks which are used are done so without consent and any use of the same does not imply consent or permission was gained from the owner. Any trademarks or brands found within are purely used for clarification purposes and no owners are in anyway affiliated with this work.

Contents

Introduction: 6

Chapter 1: Explaining the in and out differences 10

Chapter 2: When, why and how 16

Chapter 3: Audio and eBooks... 25

Chapter 4: Selling to attain passive income........................ 38

Chapter 5: Real Estate... 64

Chapter 6: Income streams... 81

Introduction:

We all strive for it. Quitting our everyday 9-5 job in search of the real meaning of life. We need more time in the day for family, friends, and sometimes even our own happiness. You could go as far as to try traveling the world on this pursuit. Realistically unless you were born into a luxurious lifestyle or have received a big inheritance chances are this is not your reality. Whether you like it or not, money is what makes the world go round. Without money you certainly will not be afforded the luxury of traveling or even dinning in some instances. While money does not guarantee happiness it sure does make a lot of things in our lives a little easier.

Today we will explore the possibilities of getting away from your typical 9-5 routine and expand on how passive income can help you achieve a new reality. No more worrying about how you will pay your electricity bill or a car payment. Saving for a child's education just became a little less stressful. Are you having to think of the possibility of moving a parent to a retirement community? All these things are life and if you are not prepared they can catch you off guard financially. Maybe you want to enjoy life to the fullest, travel and sightsee. Maybe you have wanted to splurge on a new hotrod. Whatever you goal throughout this eBook you will learn that anything is possible if you put forth the time and effort.

We will pretend that at this point you know nothing or very little about passive income. You must realize that there is some initial work involved before your income begins to accumulate as passive. Income. As with most things in life, there is hard work to put in before the reward. This work is well worth it to achieve financial freedom. Once you have put in the work you should be on to easy sailing as passive income requires little management and maintenance on your end once it is accumulating money.

We all have to learn somewhere and I am glad you have chosen this Kindle eBook to do so.

Chapter 1: Explaining the in and out differences

By definition Investopedia defines passive income as earnings one receives from rental properties, limited involvement or other endeavors where they are not materially involved. Always keep in mind that however you are earning passive income that the IRS will still require there share, as it is income taxable.

There are three main categories of income in regards to passive income. There is active income, passive income and the portfolio income.

Active income

Active income is also commonly known as earned income. This income is what the majority of all of us are used to. This is the act of providing a service and then getting paid for it. It includes wages, salaries, commissions, tips and income from being materially involved in businesses. It simply is the compensation from where you are employed. It also is the most taxed form of income. Not only is active income subject to high personal taxes it also taxable for Medicare and social security. If you had not guessed already now you know why your 'bring home pay' is easily half of what you actually make in a given timeframe.

Portfolio income

Portfolio income rather comes from investments, dividends, royalties and interests as well as capital gains. Portfolio income does not come from normal business activities. These portfolios are also taxed differently. However, it is not subjected to Medicare and social security taxes.

Passive income

In the simplest of terms passive income is defined as money consistently earned with little or no effort from you, the person receiving it. In addition to the above some of the most popular passive incomes come in the form of stocks and interest or retirement earnings. They may also be in the form of lottery winnings, capital gains or online work.

Unless you do happen to win the lottery passive income typically does not generate overnight, but it is possible.

Outsourcing your income

If you do a quick Google search you find different hubs of moneymaking activities online. These sites work to help promote something, while you sit back and relax, on your behalf. There are several different choices to choose from, how will you know which is best? You will need to figure out who your audience is. Your passive income will depend on what your market is.

You may be interested in earning income through a blog and some affiliate links. This is one of the most popular online ways to earn passive income. By starting a blog you will be writing about a topic that you already have a lot of knowledge about. If you enjoy what you are talking about it should be easy to continue to add regular content, as you will want to maintain this blog by keeping readers interested.

You can and should sign up for affiliate programs related to your topics on your blog. You will include links to those sites in your posts. If links are not your thing you can go as far as to add more visually appealing banners or ads to your page.

Blogs are one of the cheapest and easiest ways to acquire passive income. Once you get the ball rolling it should require little maintenance from you. You may blog as you wish or you may even choose to outsource new blog posts. As long as you have the banner, ads or affiliate links you should be able to watch your bank account start to grow.

Another outsourcing concept could be to dream up a type of business venture that you can outsource most of the business to other people, be it someone down the street, a specialized outsourcing company, or to someone across the ocean. What type of business you may ask? I'm glad you did, there are a lot of business that fit into this realm of possibility. Programming, web designs, graphics, marketing, copywriting, as well as your own consulting to CAD design are all business ideas that you would be able to utilize outsourcing.

Wouldn't everyone be doing this?

In the grand scheme of things you would think if it were easy everyone would be doing it. It is not easy and you have the potential to make mistakes. You have to be somewhat ambitious, write down your goals and envision reaching those milestones. You have to know what you want and simply start going after it. Financial freedom through passive income is worth the initial time investment to successfully begin a startup. If you delegate it properly by outsourcing soon you will be watching your dreams unfold before your very eyes.

Chapter 2: When, why and how

It is easy to get carried away once you have a plan in place. With these types of goals they require not only the proper planning but the right timing. I have never read a book where the Hare wins the race, it is always slow and steady that wins the race. It is time to visit your goals. With your passive income generating what are your plans for it? Do you wish to use it as a safety net in case you lose or job or a medical emergency arises? Are you planning to make big purchases in the future and you are looking ahead to how to generate these funds? Are you wanting to quit your 9-5 job and have more time with you family while still receiving a paycheck? Depending on these goals will depend on your outlook of long term priorities. I am going to go out on a limb and say there are a lot of people who are very interested in going the quit your job route. I do not blame you.

I quit.

Time to be honest. Have you ever pictured telling your boss those two magical words? No, not those words. The answer is, "I quit." Ah, you finally did it and you are feeling all kinds of emotions, mostly ranging from thrilled and excitement to all of a sudden having the pressure of the world on your shoulders. You have not lined up another job, you have little savings. What did you just do? You made a snap judgement without stopping to think properly about how your actions will affect the rest of your life.

You do not have to be a victim of a snap judgment like that example. You are in the beginning stages and starting to gather information now to set yourself up for a better future. Just knowing there are millions of reasons to quit your job and a million and one opportunities waiting for you could be all you need to know to dive right in, head first.

Again the Hare never wins the race, if you do not have a dive head first mentality it is perfectly acceptable to start off slow and steady. You will want to take some time to research your options and remain steady throughout your different business propositions. If need be keep repeating that slow and steady wins the race. Slow and steady does not mean procrastination and fear. If you have experienced any of these in the last few months please step forward. If you are growing tired of the typical 9-5, are needing to spend more time with family and friends, or even if you are stressed by the demands of your boss you need to move on your dream of a passive income strategy. By laying out your goals, plans and execution you will be taking steps in the right direction. Do not quit your 'normal' job until you feel confident in what you are doing is bringing in enough residual income to satisfy your lifestyle. Once you feel you no longer need the safety cushion of your 9-5 job feel free to finally say those words we all long to say, "I quit." Make an effort to not purposely burn any bridges along your departure, in this day and age it is not smart to turn away potential paying customers once you start up your own business.

Proven ways to make passive income

How exactly will you make money? Think of what makes you happy. What is something that you are good at? What is something you would be able to serve people with? Do not focus on something that will serve everyone, which is merely waiting for defeat in going that route. You need to find your market and niche. Something you can specialize in for a specialized group of people. Your earnings will reflect how directly you are serving this audience. The more this message resonates with that particular audience the more opportunities you will have to connect and sell.

Do not focus on picking a "hot topic" pick something that is going to last and that you will not tire of after several years.

If something has already been capitalized on, do not let that scare you off. Look it over and find any gaps that you can fill. If you can figure out a unique selling strategy you will have an advantage in a potential selling gap. What can you offer that this marketplace is lacking? Make sure you are transparent. Transparency leads to trust. If you have failed, let them know how you failed and why you got back up and tried again. You will be seen as resilient and a fighter, someone who does not easily give up. You will begin to establish relationships with those who went through the same situations or experiences. You will be relatable. People want to buy or invest in someone like themselves.

For people looking for more of a quick impact here are a few ways to acquire passive income:

CD Ladder

By building a CD Ladder it gives you the opportunity to take advantage of the best of long and short term CDs. Long term CDs have the opportunity to earn more but you will have less access to your money compared to short term CDs. Short term CDs traditionally have lower interest rates while providing you with access to your money more frequently. With a CD ladder you are combing both options, essentially gaining the best of both worlds. You combine long term earnings with your more frequent access to a percentage of your money.

Starting a ladder is a fairly simple process. To give an example pretend we have $30,000 and a three year goal. We will divide the full $30,000 evenly into three CDs. Each CD will have ascending terms and be 12 months apart. So every 12 months you will be able to access a portion of these funds, more importantly while your funds continue to mature.

The further out ladders (year two and three) have increased earning power. In this example we are only going out three years, you do have the option to grow your money more with a longer term ladder. Over the course of one year your CDs will grow. After the end of that 12 months you can choose to take your matured CD and "cash out" taking your money if need be, or you can continue on it and grow your ladder by renewing your CD. Longer terms tend to pay better rates. You will continue on your ladder and renew into a new three year CD, which is purchased at the current rates. You will repeat this step when you get to your second and third year maturity date with your CDs. When all of the original CDs have been renewed your ladder goes into autopilot. In this example the CDs will continue to renew by themselves into three year CDs. One matures each year until you choose yourself to stop it. You will again benefit from three year rates while you still have the access to a portion of your funds you may need annually.

Earn a higher interest from your savings

One of the easiest and quickest ways to increase passive income is to move your savings to a bank that pays a higher percentage on your savings. It may not sound like a lot but little things do tend to add up and after time interest rates do eventually rise.

The average savings account earns one-tenth of a percentage point of your balance according to Bankrate. Big banks do not usually offer up big rates. If higher rates are what you are after you may want to look into credit unions, online banks or a community bank.

Invest in Dividend paying stocks

Many people like this option because you can take advantage of steady payments. You can also take it as an opportunity to reinvest any dividends to continue purchasing additional shares of stock. Many dividend paying stocks are representing companies that are considered mature and financially stable stock prices for these companies may increase steadily over time while the shareholders enjoy the periodic dividend payments. A company that would pay out consistently is a company that is financially healthy and generates a consistent cash flow. Being stable is important in the world of stocks and balances.

Get cash rebates

There are many online sites that utilize the option of cash rebates. You do your online shopping as you would normally and in the meanwhile you earn a portion of your cash back on these purchases. Some view it as a discount and it quite possibly is, but there is something satisfying about getting a check in the mail to deposit directly into your own bank account.

Use cash back rewards

If you are responsible enough to pay off what you spend on your credit card every month, this may be a viable option for you. Certain credit cards offer easy income every month thanks to perks like the cash back bonuses. For example if you wanted to use your credit card to pay off monthly household expenses, you must pay off your credit card balance, you will make easy money by simply making necessary purchases. Some credit cards can offer an 8% cash rebate for purchases, which will start to add up as easy passive income.

Chapter 3: Audio and eBooks

A time has come for a new generation of reading. The notion of audio and portable electronic books at first did take some time to pick up speed but now eBooks have quickly taken rise replacing the necessity of having hard or paperback books. Places like Kindle allow these books to be accessed no matter where you are.

We often judge a book by its cover, literally. Browsing through bookstores or the grocery store aisle you may find a book that is of interest to you but something about the cover throws you off. If a book is not aesthetically pleasing to our eyes we simply may not buy it, even if the storyline or subject matter peaks our interest. With eBooks you cut that part out. You read a short introduction and right then and there make up your mind to purchase or not. The usually much cheaper price for eBooks also make this an easier decision than buying hardback. Let us not forget about having to tote around heavy books all the time. With the invention of Kindle you can have numerous books at your disposal on a light weight digital device. We will go more in-depth to the discovery of Kindle below.

You may wonder what audio and eBooks have to do with passive income. Well, because you can earn passive income off of this modern technology. There is a genuine satisfaction to seeing something you put together sell successfully.

ACX

We know that by writing your own book your personal words scroll across the pages. With audiobooks your voice tells the story best. You know the book and content better than anyone. You are familiar with the characters the subject and storyline. An audiobook is a creative way of narrating your own story. You are able to express your thoughts and feelings to your listeners. When you go through a company like ACX all of your revenue, or passive income, comes straight to you. You are able to decide how it is produced, narrated and distributed.

CreateSpace

The publishing world is ever evolving and CreateSpace is one self-publishing option you can look into. Through CreateSpace you will have access to tools and quality printing. Thousands of authors are publishing profitable work right this minute. They are not waiting for literally agents to give them the green light they are accessing distributions and the marketing strategies from CreateSpace to generate more passive income than they first imagined. CreateSpace started over a decade ago with the intention of wanting to help artists grow and be successful in this field. The great thing about CreateSpace is that it is a free tool you can take advantage of. They provide top notch publishing services to make your publishing and distribution easy.

Kindle

Amazon first released Kindle in late 2007 selling out within hours and remaining that way until late April of 2008. (Talk about missing an investment opportunity.) Kindle is now one of the world most recognized devices. There are now several different Kindles on the market to choose from in various price points.

Kindle enables users to glace through lists of titles from newspapers, magazines, eBooks and other digital media files. After browsing users can buy, download and read their purchases. The Kindle Store has content made up of over 4.6 eBooks available in the US as of July 2016.

Self-Publishing

Do not let that big number discourage you from publishing your own eBook, article or media file. Earlier we talked about finding something you can specialize in, something to fill the gap. This is also referred to as your niche. Priority number one to selling a profitable eBook is to go through the process of finding a niche. You can research current best sellers and find a niche from there.

The money you make by self-publishing a book on Kindle does not have to end there. You need to know how to use your other passive income streams to promote your book(s). Using your blog from above you can maintain a mailing list of your subscribers. Or when someone buys a book you can have a lead in option that has them fill in their personal info, thus creating a listserv for your products. Once you have their names and e-mail addresses you can send them every new promotion you have. You can promote your blog, books and even affiliated links, which we will go into more details about that later.

Every income stream will work together to create more passive income for you. By having them all work together there is less management on your end once it is all set up properly.

Outsourcing and ghostwriting

Not everyone is born with the right words to say or write. There are companies out there that hire ghostwriters to write other people's thoughts. Ghostwriters are someone behind the keyboard, they often get no credit and do the legwork for someone else to receive the accolades. Ghostwriters are hardworking, creative and talented people. They have high and strict demands to ensure that their clients get what they are paying for. If publishing your own book seems like a daunting, time consuming task you can think about hiring a ghostwriter. You simply supply them with the title of the book you would like written and some highlights to talk about. They go off of word count so make sure you specify how long you want the book to be.

Ghostwriting employment can be as short or as long as you would like it to be. You can write several books under a ghostwriter without ever meeting or talking to them face to face. They are as essentially as it is called, a ghost. There are ghostwriters at every level of talent and demand. Who you choose is up to you and what you choose to pay is your choice as well.

Ghostwriters usually make pennies on the dollar.

This is another route where you will have to spend a little bit of money upfront to make money but since the average 30 page eBook could take about a week to complete, that is money well spent to hire out and free you for something else.

Keywords

Once you have your subject, you have a well written (or outsourced) book you need to zone in on a few keywords about your book. Keywords are how readers will be able to find your book(s).

The keywords you choose have the potential to open up a new market. It can increase your foot traffic to your product page and ultimately it leads to people first being able to see and know your book is out there. People cannot and will not buy a product they simply do not know about. If you want to be a successful self-publisher you may as well get familiar with keywords.

These are the target words or key phrases that you want your eBook to rank high in when someone inputs these words into a search. You will need something somewhat generic to get the kind of traffic you need. You also cannot be too vague where your book describes how to purchase your first house but it is pulling up under searches about Pluto. There is a fine middle line you must follow.

Some words get a lot more traffic than other words. There are a few popular keywords that get a lot less competition however. You will want to utilize these keywords. Amazon allows you to use 7 keywords before uploading your book. These keywords help Amazon to figure out the algorithm in where your book will show up on the list of results. There are also SEO (Search Engine Optimization) keywords which also tend to be more universal. These are important because it goes outside of just the

Amazon search engine to include Google, Yahoo and others. This is important in driving more outside traffic to your sales page. Unlike Amazon SEO keywords are not officially selected by you and listed under keywords. You will need to identify your SEO keywords and use them strategically throughout your page. You may want to insert these keywords into your Book title, subtitle, introduction, or even the summary.

Final stages

You are nearing the final stages of becoming a full fledge eBook self-publisher which means you are one step closer to achieving your goal of passive income. With CreateSpace you first need to sign up for an account. You add a new title, taking you to the start a new project page. Once there you will fill in all the pertinent information about your eBook. CreateSpace is a useful tool because it also walks you through each and every step. After you successfully upload your book you will go through the process of choosing a cover. Review your book, choose your distribution channels, and set a competitive price and lastly write a short description. You have successful self-published your first eBook.

If you go the Kindle option now is when you will want to upload your book. Kindle has their own direct publishing platform which can be overwhelming looking at the instructions. Once you take a deep breath and clear your head you realize it is pretty simple. Log in using your Amazon account, enter your personal information and begin the process of uploading your content. Publishing should take less than 5 minutes and within 24-48 hours your book should be available on Kindle worldwide. Sit back and watch your passive income grow.

Audiobooks

If you are hesitant to go the eBook route give audiobooks a try. ACX has low production rates so you have more passive income in your pocket. ACX manages audiobooks through Amazon, iTunes and Audible, all which have been to be proven industry leaders. With ACX you also have the option of being your own narrator or hiring someone to narrate for you. For either option you will take the above tools from your book to serve as your script. Title, book description and summary, you will speak all of this into your audiobook. You could even hire someone to do it for you. To hire a narrator you can use portions of your book as a script for auditions. Once you have your narrator selected you need to find a producer. You can also use samples of your book as an audition for the producer role. Review your candidates and make an offer. If the producer accepts your offer you have now officially made a deal on ACX. The producer will record a 15 minute checkpoint. At this point you will be able to provide feedback and approve the process thus far. Once the sample has been approved your producer will continue recording until the project is completed. Once your audiobook is completed and you are happy with services rendered you will pay your producer (unless you agreed upon a royalty agreement) and lastly you are ready to distribute your audiobook. You have now finished your first audiobook and with your successful completion your passive income will begin to grow.

No matter what book option you choose to go through you need to know how to market and maintain positive reviews for your book. Hiring a virtual assistant will help do this work for you. Virtual assistants, or VA's, can help with any part of the workload. They not only can take on the task of gathering reviews for your own book but they can help to market your book as well. They can help to complete research or contact bloggers to promote the book. They may participate in giving honest reviews of your book on-line. You may want their help in setting up a distribution list where you can send your book in favor of getting feedback or reviews. Ultimately hiring a VA will leave you with more free time to look into other opportunities to acquire passive income.

Chapter 4: Selling to attain passive income

This is one of the longest chapters in this eBook. I warn you because it also has a lot of crucial information you do not want to miss. Part of passive income is about the opportunity to sell or market what you already know. Below are several different ways to achieve this.

If you have not heard of Amazon you either are simply living under a rock or have no interest in on-line shopping. Amazon is the largest internet based retailer not just in the United States but also in the world. These facts are based upon market capitalization and total sales. (Another missed investment opportunity I would venture to guess.) Amazon headquarters are located in Seattle, Washington. Interestingly enough Amazon started its business as an online bookstore. It quickly grew to selling DVDs, audiobooks, software and video games, to electronic, apparel and home furnishings. Amazon has branded itself as a convenient one stop shop.

Fulfilment by Amazon

With Fulfilment by Amazon or FBA you can store products through Amazon's fulfilment center. They do all the manual work, or take heavy lifting quite literally. They will pick out your products, pack and ship to the customers as well as provide any customer service in regards to your products. Amazon will boost your sales because they have the tools and manpower to help fulfil your orders on demand.

Prior to setting up a sellers account on Amazon you will need to find and manufacture a profitable product. The initial amount you want to invest is entirely up to you. If you research correctly and are buying and selling the right products at the right prices you should be making sales and gaining profits in no time.

Once you have your product and are producing your goods now is the time to set up that sellers account on Amazon. Create your product listing(s). Amazon has a catalog where you can add products one at a time or in bulk. Be sure your products are prepared and well-made to be shipped safely and securely all over the world into your customer's hands.

Now that you've completed those steps you want to create shipping plans. Engage in a discounted carrier plan. Amazon's partnered carrier is UPS. They offer deeply discounted rates and the cost is billed directly to you. They even go as far as to provide shipping labels that you can print when you use their carrier. Ship and track your shipments to Amazon's fulfilment centers. Amazon also offers a sellers tool to help you with any questions throughout this process, so rest assured that it is not as daunting as it sounds.

You have come this far now it is time to get down to the nitty gritty of making money. Customers will have the ability to order your product(s) online. If a customer is an Amazon

Prime member they will get fast, free shipping on all your products. Amazon also allows customers to qualify for free shipping on eligible orders if they do not choose to be a prime member. Amazon fills orders efficiently and quickly using an advanced web to warehouse sorting system. Customers always receive tracking information from Amazon. There is a peace of mind in knowing where in the buying and shipping stages your product is at.

Lastly, Amazon will take care of providing customer support for the products you sell. They offer world class customer service and their team manages customer questions, feedback, refunds, inquiries and returns 24 hours a day, 365 days a year.

Amazon is a great opportunity to capitalize on passive income at its finest. You make a well-made, sought after product and let Amazon take over the rest. Enjoy the rewards of your hard work while you move on to your next product or project.

Informational products and online courses

Are people really making a living by maintaining a successful informational product business? The answer is yes. There are several product business on the market today. At the end of this you just may have some ideas of your own to dream up.

Believe it or not you can create an online course as a good way to acquire passive income. You simply teach something once and get paid for it over and over again. These may have the potential to be perceived as more valuable than eBooks because you can set up a weekly or daily distribution list and can generally turnover more product quicker than going through the process of an eBook. People tend to check their emails on a more consistent basis, up to several times a day. If you are sending out courses via a listserv the chances of you staying relevant and connecting with those who find your courses useful will play in your favor for gaining that passive income. They will find your courses useful and continue to subscribe. They also are able to recommend you to their family and friends. Do not underestimate the power of word of mouth recommendations. If someone is happy with a product they want to share a positive encounter with family, friends and coworkers. On the other hand if someone is not happy with a product or service they also will not hesitate to warn others to stay clear. That is why it is important to maintain transparency and sell well made products.

YouTube

If you tend to think an on-line course is too serious for your nature you can look into getting your own YouTube. Gone are the days of YouTube being used only for young kids doing tricks off their bikes or fun dives into their pool. YouTube is now a relevant source for video tutorials and ecommerce. YouTube has turned into the second most popular search engine used to find a fix-it-fast solution or for do it yourself projects.

 A study showed that 6 billion hours was the total time people spent watching YouTube, a month. That is a lot of views, totaling about half an hour a person, in the world. For you that could mean a lot of viewers brining big opportunities and even bigger business. Through this on-line marketing tool you have the ability to have branding and traffic at your literal fingertips.

To set up your own YouTube channel you will first need to start with a video recorder. You can start with a webcam and work your way up to a digital camera or a full fledge high definition camcorder. Once you have figured out how you will broadcast what you are selling you need to invest in a good microphone. It is important that they can hear what you are selling just as much as they need to see you. This will have a big impact on your video quality. If it looks like you are shooting a quick blurb down in your mother's basement no one is going to take you, your product or channel seriously. There are several good quality mics for every budget. To try to avoid giving your audience sea sickness watching your videos you will want to stabilize your camcorder or digital camera by using a tripod so your video runs smoothly and not bumping all around.

Next invest in some simple lighting to avoid overhead shadows. Conventional lighting can look cheap and add shadows that will not benefit your video. If you want to go one step further you can add a backdrop to your video. You can mix up fabric colored backgrounds for different character and ambiance. Photography background support stands and fabrics to match should not run you a lot of money and your investment will pay off with your professional looking video.

Point, shoot, record. That is all you should need to sell a product or sell your tutorials on YouTube. In the chance that you will need to edit a video you also may want to invest in some editing software. There is no need for it to be extensive as you should only have to do minor edits for your channel.

Once your channel is up and running you again need to decide what product or tutorial you will be selling. You can add extra videos to your channel such a question and answer section. Most consumers will have some questions either before or after they buy. You question and answers area could boost your sales by tipping the scales if someone was leery on whether they were going to purchase your product or not. You also will seem highly proactive by putting these out there before they need to be asked. Probably, most importantly, it will save you time by not having to answer the same questions day in and day out.

A YouTube channel tip is to fil some behind the scenes videos. These seem to do very well, especially in regards to branding on YouTube. If you make your own product(s) it may not be a bad idea to show the detailed process of manufacturing. It not only gives your viewers reassurance that they are buying quality products it will reassure your buyers of your business practice.

You may be worried that a question and answer segment as well as implementing a behind the scenes video will have a limited audience. If you are worried about that, experiment with topical content. Topical content is focused on helping viewers find a solution to a problem. Topical content has the potential to reach thousands more in viewers. You can even focus on trivia facts or random knowledge. Anything to keep customers engaged and involved will keep them coming back for more. If you sell clothes you can show your subscribers easy ways to pack clothing for a trip. Better yet, you can give them a list of the must have clothing essentials to pack for vacation.

Real people and honest feedback speak volumes of your product. How do these people use what you are selling? How do they like it? How has it helped them? You can interview these customers and with their permission share their stories on your channel.

This probably all sounds exciting until you start thinking about how you will generate the traffic to your channel. Fortunately for you, YouTube has multiple methods offered to let viewers interact.

Annotations are the cream of the crop when it comes to YouTube marketing. You can use them as a call-to-action at different places within your video. Ideally you should try to have one at the beginning, middle and at the end. Best of all you can link this to any other videos on your channel.

A video description is sometimes overlooked as a method to get clicks and leads. The description should include various links to your page as well as the description of your video. Make sure you are using keywords that you learned about earlier.

The best way to generate traffic to your page or channel is to promote your channel. A simple way to promote something is to engage your viewers. If you are making good use of your question and answer videos you should already have well engaged viewers. You can also answer comments on your videos as well as other videos of similar topics. Be wary of pushing your products aggressively on these other videos. Instead you want to subtly drop hints that the other commenter can learn more about you and your product on your own channel. You are supposed to be helpful first, selling will follow.

You can promote your channels outside of YouTube. You can message your friends to help spread the word of your channel as well as generate views by contacting relevant bloggers and newspaper outlets to share our videos. Do not forget about sharing and posting your YouTube channel on your invoices and with shipping information that you send out with product orders.

To promote within the YouTube community you can create another segment asking for people if they would subscribe to your channel. You can insert a segment or phrase at the end of every video with the above learned annotation that can point to the subscribe button. It is important to brand your channel. You can use a brand image in the channel header and fill in the about section with info about your brand.

Selling on YouTube will require some time commitment up. By taking the time to create and successfully run a YouTube channel it will further open up opportunities to help you implement these designs to sell and advertise your product.

Stock photos

With the invention of digital photography there has been an increase in the amount of people who take photographs as a way to document their way of life. Babies being born, birthday parties, date nights, simple walks to the park these all have been long documented to show people how we are living.

Photography can be a job, hobby or simply a stream of passive income waiting for you to discover. All you need to do is understand what people are looking for and what you need to do to capitalize on that niche.

It is simple to take one of your photos and sell is as a stock photo to contribute to a brochure, website or product advertisement. More than likely the photos that you see in these forms are taken by people just like you and more than likely are not professionally taken.

A stock photo is something taken as an image, licensed and then used for multiple purposes. There is the advantage of you to do something once and it being able to continue to create passive income for you. A magazine hires someone to take specific pictures based upon articles or things in the news; a model for a clothing line for a feature in women's wear. Stock photos are the complete opposite. Say you take a breathtaking sunrise picture. You may upload that picture into a stock photo house who is essentially a broker to potential clients, using your photo. Your photo has the potential to get used once, twice, ten or tens of thousands of times.

The stock house and the photographer (you) receive money each time a client uses your image. Depending on your negotiated price and stock house fees you could come out potentially making a great deal of income. The great part about this strategy is that you can make money day or night, while you are awake or even while you are sleeping. Once uploaded to the stock house people can access it anytime. If you have a nice selection of stock photos to choose from you could possibly wake up to $5, $50 or $5,000 in one night's sleep. There are endless possibilities when it comes to stock photos.

To start in stock photography you need to attain a collection of good quality pictures that clients would want to use. If you personally have a lot of interest in a certain picture a potential client may have no use for something you view as a good or quirky photo. They will buy what they have use for. If the photograph is out of focus, blurry or not well done the stock house may reject it before the client can.

Next, you need to find a well reputable stock broker for photos to distribute the work. A good photography broker will have a lot of tips and pointers for specifics in what their clientele is looking for. They will be a tremendous help in telling you how to take better photographs and even assisting with technical questions. Be sure you compare different terms and payout rates. You can sign up to be an exclusive distributor if you will only plan to use one photo broker. If you plan on licensing photos to other sites or brokers you do not want to sign up as an exclusive contributor. In doing so you may be hindering your overall income potential. It is generally more valuable to sign up among several various sites and to distribute your work though those different channels.

Do not take a rejection personally. Not every picture taken by every person will make the cut. Stock houses want to make money. The only way they continue to make money is by putting the best of the best in front of their clients. You need images of the highest quality. Figure out the useful aspect of a stock photo from the perspective of the client, do not bank on getting approval just because you think it is a good, well taken photo.

Take your time to read the copyright agreements. All stock houses are different and their terms will be different as well. Read the fine print before you sign or agree to anything.

You must understand your rights that you will have to attain the photos. There could be a possibility that you will not have any rights once you turn over your photos to licensing. You want to avoid getting into a situation where you, the photographer, are not personally allowed to use your own photo because you have agreed to those terms already. Make sure you understand any legalities before you sign and commit yourself.

Lastly, realize you will not have the ability to control or an opinion on your photo. You may have taken a picture of your handsome graduate but the advertisers in charge deem it worthy of a medical ointment or domestic abuse campaign. That could lead to some awkward conversations or embarrassing moments. To avoid that you could stick to natural, generic content. That way no matter how it is intended to be used, it should not cause any problems and you can continue to have revenue in your bank account.

Drop shipping

Drop shipping is simply cutting out the middle work. It is a fulfilment model allowing you to buy bulk or individual products from a wholesaler and have them shipped directly to your customers' doorsteps. This cuts out the work you would need to purchase a large amount of readily available inventory and then you would need to think of where you would store all these products. Most people have warehouses for inventory. Warehouses require space, electricity, running water, workers, heavy duty machinery and more overhead. With this model you simply partner with a supplier and list their merchandise for sale. Once you get an order you forward it to the supplier to fulfill. The supplier ships the product from their warehouse, where they are paying for space, electricity and workers to run the machinery, to your customers. They charge you for the price of the shipped item only. This is a model not too far away from Amazon FBA product model we discussed earlier. The difference in Drop shipping is that you do not have to invest thousands of your own money into inventory. Instead you only buy a product when there is an existing order to fill. When you do not have to pre-buy all your inventory you want to sell, you can offer a wider number of products to your buyers. Without a significant number invested in inventory the risks that are usually involved in starting an online store are greatly reduced. If things were to not work out with your business you would still be stuck with thousands in inventory and even more thousands less in income. You may have to sell at a loss. As discussed earlier you can rest without the stress of having to run a warehouse for all of your inventory. Drop shipping operates from any space equipped with laptops or computers. All you need is a reliable internet connection.

It is possible to create a drop shipping business and be extremely profitable. There is no magic formula, it will take effort, significant energy and time but it is a business opportunity that takes little risk and pays off with great options for passive income. Your income will be based on your specific niche, dedication and commitment. Hard work is an approach you should mentally prepare for when you want to start the process of beginning to tackle a drop ship business model. Once your business is up and running it can pretty much operate itself for most of the day to day activity of the business.

People use drop shipping for products everywhere. The most popular sits and eBay and Shopify.

eBay

eBay is another hugely popular online marketplace. It brings people together all over the world to buy or sell almost anything. eBay works by a seller listing an item on the site. From Antiques, books, cars to sporting goods you can find it all on eBay. The seller will choose to accept only bids much like an auction, or they can choose the buy it now option. Buy it now offers buyers the opportunity to buy now, straight away at the fixed price with no negotiation. In the bidding, or auction, option the bidding opens generally at a low price and the seller will specific how long the bidding will take place for. Potential buyers place bids against each other for the certain item. When the listing expires the person with the highest (last) bid wins the item. Buying and selling in this fashion is easy and if you like a challenge can even be fun.

Drop shipping on popular sites like eBay Shopify are options to attaining passive income.

Shopify

Shopify is a solution to drop shipping and is common among ecommerce business. Much like eBay you set up an online store to sell your product. With Shopify you not only organize your items but you also are able to customize your storefront as well. This site is set up to take your credit card payment and you can track and respond to your orders, all just by a few clicks of your mouse. Since this is an ecommerce software and solely web based it means you do not have to install anything, it works and is compatible with various different operating systems. They take all the guess work out of running an online store. You set up your storefront and generate revenue. They offer a 14 day free trial to get accustomed to Shopify. After the trial they offer various different pricing plans to best suit your nature and size of your business.

Affiliate Marketing

If you simply do not think you have the ability to create a product that would generate sales or want to keep expanding on your passive income you can look into affiliate marketing. This is the process of earning a commission based upon promoting other people's products. You also have the option to promote business products as well. Finding something you like tends to be easy enough to want to promote, so that would be your first step. Find a product you like. Promote it. Earn part of the profit based upon each sale you make.

There are certain tips and tricks you should know about when it comes to affiliate marketing. Affiliate marking starts with relationships. When someone you know recommends a product, really stop and listen to what they are saying. Pay attention to the key words they are speaking. Be sincere and trustworthy in all you do, especially online. This will lay a foundation of having effective affiliate marketing skills.

Any of your online tools from above will be a great resource in affiliate marketing. Focus on getting more traffic. More traffic means more people to potentially buy what you are promoting. If you are already using something promote that first. That may seem like a no brainer, but if you are using specialized lighting for your YouTube channel, that would be an easy first promotion. Look at what you are doing, look at what you already have around you, start with those first.

Make sure you always promote wisely and do not be afraid to be honest. Talk about what you liked and what you did not. Talk about what has worked and about what could have been done better. It may not pad your pockets right away, but going back up to trust being key, it will pay off in the long run. You can be honest and truthful without having to be negative. You may want to think twice before you begin bashing a product or person you are supposed to be promoting. It may be wise to contact the company prior to your review and let them know your thoughts and see if they can improve on a product first. We all have not so perfect days, maybe you simply received something off, and you can be a person who believes in second chances still embark on honest reviews.

In choosing products you would like to review or promote choose products that will help your followers solve a problem or even could address a potential fear. These tend to be excellent choices as people shy away from purchases of the unknown. If you make them feel comfortable in understanding something better they will be more likely to make a purchase. It is also important to know your audience, you can realistically know what they will buy. If the people following you are dog lovers you may not want to stick to reviewing the best kitty litter on the market, I would guess those sales may not go in your favor.

Another important tip, is to know how much they are willing to spend. Know who your network is. If your network is a comprised of people without a lot of disposable income there are slimmer chances you will get them to shell out $50 for a top of the line chew toy for their pets.

You may want to avoid promoting around the holidays. Does your audience tend to take vacations from their computers around this time? Or maybe that is the time you should promote as people may be looking for big deals and sales around holidays. It boils down to knowing who your audience is. Get to know them and they will tell you all you need to know to promote to your best advantage.

If you still have your virtual assistant around you can have them do some affiliated marketing on your audio or eBooks. Sure, they will get some of your profit but by their legwork your sales will increase, thus resulting in more money gains and again more time on your hands to jump into another adventure.

Chapter 5: Real Estate

By now you have learned a lot of online selling hacks. You may not think real estate and online selling go hand in hand but you will quickly learn they have more in common than you may have first thought.

Few investments or sales mechanisms have made a big impact on becoming wealthy as with real estate. There are two ways to invest in real estate. First you can do a direct purchase of a property or there is an option to invest through an indirect mean.

Going the direct purchase route generally requires a larger upfront costs but in general you should also have the potential for higher investment returns. If you choose to do an indirect investment those are usually made through a real estate investment trust or REIT. You can also establish an indirect investment through a tax lien but it will not involve the direct or immediate ownership of the property.

In regards to attaining passive income we will focus on the market of real estate rentals. If you want to look at other options for income you may want to do some further research into buying and remodeling a house in order to resale at a higher price or solely for a profit. Usually flipping a house requires a lot more work and funds than what real estate investors are wanting to put out to offset their passive income.

Like with most topics we have already covered the potential of income can fall into a wide range of possibilities depending on how you approach your strategy. Know how much you are willing to spend and most importantly know yourself and how happy you will be to embark on a project like with real estate investment. Learn what you can do for yourself and what you will need to hire out to do. It will take away from your cash flow at the beginning but it will also push you closer to truly having passive income.

Get familiar with all the moving parts of a real estate business. Before you clear your calendar and dump all your money into a project ask yourself a few key questions. Do you want to rent out residential or commercial properties? Buying and renting commercial space for offices, retail or industrial space will generally give you a lower return but it may yield far lower headaches down the road. Another drawback may be it that it costs a lot more to buy one property with commercial space. If you plan to go with residential real estate what is the type of economical neighborhood you are searching for? Do you plan to aim for a lower income neighborhood, fix up the house and rent for higher? Do you prefer to go to a higher income area and potentially have less turnover with tenants, but not bring in as much passive income keeping up with the higher monthly payments? You should look for houses that you would feel comfortable yourself living in. If your business does not take off as fast or as successfully as you were hoping you may have no option but to live in the house yourself.

Start off small. Find a house you could picture you or your family living in. Find something that needs minor or low maintenance repairs. Make sure the repairs are something that you would feel comfortable doing. Look for any updates you can make by making cosmetic changes first. New carpet and a fresh coat of paint can instantly make a house look more marketable and less lived in. Most average people can complete these on their own, which means a lot less money out of your pocket upfront.

Once you have learned as much as you can about what you need to look for in the real estate business, and you have begun to use that information to find your first house now you can look into options to get the business properly financed.

Financing your real estate investments

Few people, especially just starting out, are able to pay all cash for properties. Besides gaining your own passive income a big benefit to a real estate investment business model is that you are able to buy property on borrowed money. You are then also able to write off any interest on your taxes as a business expense.

Most new investors to real estate take out a conventional mortgage for their first property. They put down a 10% to 30% down payment. Higher down payments tend to decrease your monthly payment it will increase your immediate cash flow, but it will also likely reduce a return on the money you put up.

With a sound credit score you should be able to obtain a conventional mortgage, regardless your interest rates will possibly be higher on rental properties than an owner occupied home loan. If you are unable to obtain a loan to maintain the mortgage on the property you may still have some options in your favor, though there is a high probability that rates will be a lot higher. You could try to approach the seller personally. They may be willing to sell or finance the property through monthly installments. Or you may want to look into the possibility of bringing in a partner to finance the money. This is not always a feasible option for new investors with little to no experience and no real connections to the market, but it can be an option for the future. Once you build your portfolio you can begin to rethink this as it will be easier to work with people you have built connections and maintained relationships with during business expeditions. Money partners have the ability to lend based upon a rate basis or with a portion of the profits, they can even do a combination of the two.

Finding properties

Moving right along. There are a lot of ways to find different properties to help grow your investment business. MLS (Multiple Listing Service) are one of the most popular and widely used ways to search for specific requirements as real estate agents use this as a platform to advertise and promote their listings. As you continue to grow you may build and explore different relationships with real estate agents who will want to give you a good lead on a potential house for sale. Make sure you are extremely clear about what you want and hopefully they will be selective in what they are showing you. They are not showing you a "steal" just to try and get a quick sale out of you. You need to make sure you are buying a good house, not necessarily just a house at a great deal. Sometimes a cheap house will end up being a big money pit for you down the road, do your homework before you decide upon a steal. If you are unsure on an agents motives you can look up the banks REO (real estate owned) page. These are foreclosed homes that the banks own and often are the best source of value as the price is listed on right there on the banks page. You may be able to negotiate a better price than listed on the REO. A similar option to look at are sheriff's sale properties. These are generally managed through the county treasurer's or sheriff's office. Typically they will have some sort of judgement against them, generally being the foreclosure notice that goes right before the bank REO is sent out.

If bank foreclosures and liens sound like a huge headache you may look into the possibility of finding properties that are not currently for sale. You possibly will need some investigation skills on your end to find the owners of run down or completely abandoned properties. In doing some leg work you may uncover a great deal without the headache or hassle with competition from other investors.

After you have an address go to your county's assessor page on the internet and locate the owner's information. This page is a great tool to also finding out the assessed home value, previous sale records and specific house measurements and characteristics. Even the worst run down looking house could be a great deal for the right price. You will not know that until you know how much the property is worth to know if the price is indeed right. There are different ways to value a property but the two most popular are comparable sales and capitalization rate approaches.

Comparable sales

The approach for comparable sales is valuing the property against similar properties in the area that have recently sold. Write down the specific characteristics of the property including the age, square footage, the number of bed and bathrooms, what is the neighborhood like as well as certain features, does it come with central air or a manual garage. Is the basement finished or unfinished. Once you have your property specifics you need to obtain the specifics on the homes that recently sold in the area to compare statistics. You will want to compare at least ten sales to get a good idea of the average value for the targeted property. If your county assessor is up to date on all this information this process will be fairly simple.

To compare properties set a range for your search. Unless you are looking in a cookie cutter neighborhood most houses are not exactly the same square footage and description. Look for properties within 15 years of each other and within a few hundred feet or so in square footage, but do try to keep it as similar as you can.

Once you have a working list to compare divide the selling price by the square footage to figure out the homes price per square footage. Do this for each comparable property. Once you have each of the properties average price per square foot make a list from most expensive to least expensive. Using the average price per square footage from your list you can find the target value of your property.

Capitalization rate

Using the capitalization rate approach to value a property may not give you the most accurate true market rate, but it is however, a lot more straightforward. A cap rate is the annual net operating income, also known as NOI. You take the cap rate of the property and divide it by the cost or value. NOI is the amount left after all expenses are paid, before any taxes or interest payments. Simply the cap rate equals annual net operating income/property value. With the cap rate formula there are two ways to look at it. If you know the type of return you are hoping to achieve or have the average return on comparable properties then you can find the approximate value by dividing the NOI by the required return. You can also take the NOI and divide it by the asking price to estimate what kind of a return you would get on the sale without negotiating at a better price.

It may seem like a lot of unneeded work but knowing the approximate value of a potential property is the first step in getting the best deal. You should not be afraid in asking for a lower price or be afraid to haggle or negotiate for a better price. The absolute worst decision you could make is to feel rushed or bullied into a sale to only find out later that you grossly overpaid. Go into your negotiations with a set, maximum price and a starting offer. Go from there on your options to wiggle towards the final price.

Finding tenants

Here is where your online selling tools finally come in handy. You may simply want to advertise a sale by hanging it in a window, or you can generate more views by using your online skills to post on-line. There are countless search engines to place these ads in. These sites tend to be fairly cheap as well as giving the people the comfort of shopping from their own homes while admiring yours.

Do not rush into an agreement to fill a vacant house and suffer long term with bad tenants throughout the lease. Thoroughly review their tenant application, run a credit check as well as a criminal background check. Good credit and clean records do not guarantee smooth sailing but it is a great way to start. Bad tenants may end up trashing your property and costing you more in missed rent and eviction costs, not to mention the legality of a potential mess on your hands. It may not be a bad idea to drive by where the hopeful tenants are currently living. If they are not taking care of their current property, chances are they will not likely take care of yours.

When you feel comfortable with your chosen tenants living in your house make sure they understand the rules and regulations and then make sure they understand it again. Familiarize yourself with how an eviction process takes place and have your own policy for the chance that you may need it. Hopefully you do not, but it will come to your legal aid if you should have to proceed with an eviction.

Maintenance

We have not talked much about how to receive your passive income with regards to a real estate investment up until now. That is because with most passive income options there is the legwork that must come first. Once you have picked and bought your property or properties depending on how ambitious you are feeling, you have found respectable tenants you can now work out how you will acquire your passive income.

Depending on how many properties you bought and your past experience with home improvement or maintenance you may be able to take care of these steps yourself. More than likely you will not be able to fix everything solely yourself, it may be beneficial to find a good plumber or electrician that you can contract out odd jobs to come and do. You may find it easier and have a more hands off approach and hire a general maintenance person to take over these problems.

Your cash flow, or passive income will come after all the expenses and tax liabilities have been paid for the month. Any leftover is yours to disperse as you wish. This passive income strategy may be one of the most expensive start up options but it also has the potential to turn into one of the biggest acquisitions of steady cash flow once you start paying off properties. You can look forward to each check that gets mailed to you becoming almost all an instant profit. Your income will also continue to grow as you become more familiar with this process and grow more efficient with your time and management to acquire more properties.

Vacation rentals

If staying local does not excite you how about beautiful beaches or stunning sunsets over snowcapped mountains? Airbnb is an online marketing place where people can find, list and rent their vacation homes. It has over 1,500,000 listings all over the world and 60,000,000 guests. It connects travelers looking for vacation rentals to rent. Sticking to passive income and vacation rentals you have a few options. You could sign up to become an Airbnb host. Airbnb prides itself on both host and guests being real people with real homes. It is a trusted place for people to list and discover unique accommodations from around the world. They have several different price points and have a world class customer service and ever growing community of users and hosts.

With Airbnb you could find it easy to utilize your extra space to obtain passive income or you may choose to use some of our rental property investments as an option. By listing your investment properties you stay along the same lines of what you would do for a yearly or monthly contracted tenant with a few exceptions.

Some fun exceptions could be that you get to meet a variety of people from all over the world. Depending on how many bedrooms you have you could make each room a different theme. You could also turn the property into more of a bed and breakfast and allow for multiple guests at the same time, streamlining more profit for the same property.

You will also need to think about how you will do the upkeep on a vacation rental. Do you prefer to do all the work yourself? You may want to rethink having a maintenance person as you may receive calls or odd ball jobs at any hour of the day or night. You may also want to look into hiring a staff, as you will running a small hosting business of sorts. You will want someone or a professional cleaning service to come in and make sure the house is up to par for your next arrival of guests. If your property is not local you will want to look into a trusted real estate company who can look over your property and maintain a copy of your key for your guests. All these things will require more money up front and possibly on a continual basis from you. With a site like Airbnb being based upon reviews and customer satisfaction you will want to go above and beyond to maintain a perfect score to ensure you continue to book your properties, thus continuing your steady stream of income straight into your bank account.

Chapter 6: Income streams

We have talked about endless potentials for you to obtain passive income. Some options seem a lot easier than others. Some goals require much more work but the payoffs are much more rewarding. The great thing about passive income is that once you put in the leg work at the beginning there is not much you have to do to keep it going. The good news for you is that you can be involved in as many different diverse income streams as you would want to be.

It may seem overwhelming at first, but by starting with the easiest stream it is completely doable by building upon each successful business. In starting with the easiest option first it also may help to break you out of your comfort shell and move into a different business strategy from where you have been before. Start with blogging or Kindle publishing first.

After you are successfully doing some side work save up some extra money for an emergency fund. In that fund could be money set aside to start your next diverse business expenditure. If you have quite a bit of debt you could also use this passive income to pay down some of those debts.

Once you are finding your footing and getting comfortable look into Amazon's FBA strategy and test your hands in the selling waters. Airbnb and real estate investing are an ambitious goal and probably requires the biggest and most expensive investments. Those results do not mean they fall short of any passive income goals you have set for yourself, but you can turn that into more of a long term goal or as a last option with passive income.

The benefit with putting effort into multiple active streams is because you can't tell the future. If one of those streams were to dry up you would be left without that income. If you have multiple, diverse income streams you will continue to be ok. The reason for diversity is just that as well. If you put all your eggs in one basket, so to speak, you never know if that is the stream that will cease to exist. Shooting all your passive income down the drain rather than just one faucet of your streams. When all streams are up and going you should be bringing in more than you are spending, paying off debts and properties and creating more passive income down the road.

Unlimited potential

Now is the time we have come full circle. What was it that you were striving for at the beginning? Quitting your 9-5 job in search of the real meaning of life, family, friends and happiness? Maintaining your passive income gives you the opportunity to actually do all that and more. If your income streams work properly you may find yourself asking what you will do to occupy all your free time. You will have passive income to not only quit your job but to fund your traveling of find genuine happiness.

Passive income gives us the ability to do all the things we only wish we had time for. Everyone needs money. Most money comes being earned. Most earnings come from hard work. Now you are equipped with the tools and tips to go out and make the best of your own talent and skills. We are all born with these special gifts and it is up to us to find out what we are good at and to make a living with it. In your case, you can make several livings from it.

The two worst things you can do in regards to passive income is to wait and to not try. Waiting is missed income. You may want to wait a year to really let everything sink in, but in that year Joe down the street has started 4 different diverse income streams and is starting to pay off debt to start another business. If you let fear stop you from trying you will never go anywhere in life. No one ever succeeded without first trying. We cannot speak defeat into ourselves before we even begin to try. You build things. If something works continue to do it until it does not work anymore. You never know, by that time you may have found a more efficient way to get something to work and then you can continue on the cycle. All the while, your income continues to climb if you simply first try.

Ask yourself if what you are doing is just for the money. If your customers or audience sense you are only in this for the money then you have a high probability of not succeeding. Your intentions should drive you in the right direction so pay attention to what those intentions are. Nothing is wrong with achieving passive income but you do not want to push future business away in that being the only thing you are focused on.

Continue to build your platform. Do not stop sharing your passion and your message, be it on a podcast, blog or your YouTube channel. You do not need to serve everyone, you only need to serve your audience.

Whatever path you choose to financial freedom just remember the path is not always straight and narrow it is often times a jumbled up puzzle that you will have to continue to navigate towards, using different skillsets and monopolizing on different strategies. Keep your eyes focused on your long term goals to succeed and you may even wonder why you did not start sooner.

Thank you for reading this book, I hope you enjoyed it and now have enough clarity on how you can attain passive income to improve your life.

If you enjoyed this book you may also be interested in checking out my book Shopify: Beginner to Pro Guide which is also available on Amazon.

https://www.amazon.com/dp/B01ISNMF30

www.ingramcontent.com/pod-product-compliance
Lightning Source LLC
Chambersburg PA
CBHW060407190526
45169CB00002B/788